Extension Textbook

D1304971

Heinemann is an imprint of Pearson Education Limited, a company incorporated in England and Wales, having its registered office at Edinburgh Gate, Harlow, Essex, CM20 2JE. Registered company number: 872828

Heinemann is a registered trademark of Pearson Education Limited

Writing team
John T Blair
Percy W Farren
Myra A Pearson
John W Thayers
David K Thomson

First Published 2002

10 09
13 12 11

ISBN 978 0 435178 76 5

Typeset by Mandy Emery.
Illustrated by David Till and David Kearney.
Cover Illustation by Mark Oliver.
Printed and bound in China (CTPS / 11)

Contents

The ancient Egyptians used hieroglyphic symbols to record numbers.

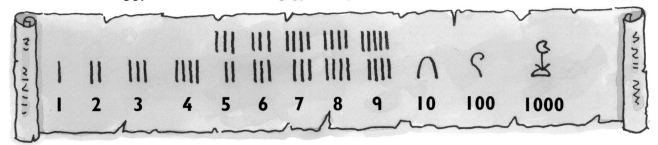

1   Write numbers for these hieroglyphics.

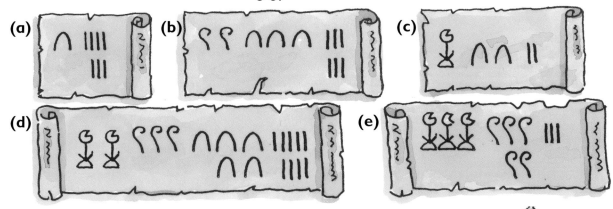

(a)

(b)

(c)

(d)

(e)

2   Write these numbers using hieroglyphic symbols.

(a) 14   (b) 48   (c) 161   (d) 2085

3   Write, using hieroglyphic symbols:

(a) the number of children in your class
(b) the number of days in a leap year
(c) the year of your birth.

4   Those parchments show how many stones and logs were used by two teams helping to build a pyramid.

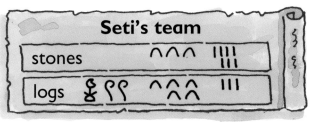

For Amun's and Seti's teams, find
(a) the total number of   • stones   • logs
(b) the difference between the numbers of   • stones   • logs.

1 (a) What was the total amount of *Lucky Lotto* prizemoney paid to the Browns and the Greens?

(b) How much more prizemoney was paid to the Greens than the Browns?

2 Find • each total • each difference.

(a) £3 624 132   £9 570 295   **(b)** £8 604 700   £6 102 937

(c) £269 079   £7 493 578   **(d)** £10 908 020   £9 164 351

3 • The total amount of money raised by *Lucky Lotto* ticket sales in two months was £25 916 254.
• The total amount paid out as prizemoney was £18 491 372.
• £3 634 535 was given to charities.

(a) What was the difference between the amount of prizemoney paid and the amount given to charities?

(b) How much **profit** did *Lucky Lotto* make in the two months?

Topside Council
Homes for rent

Homes for rent	Rent per month
Flat	£197
Terraced house	£219
Semi-detached house	£248
Small detached house	£275
Large detached house	£313

1 How much rent should Topside Council collect from each group of homes in
   • one month • one year?

(a) 48 flats
(b) 36 terraced houses
(c) 32 semi-detached houses
(d) 28 small detached houses
(e) 21 large detached houses

2 Topside Council decides to build a range of new homes on some empty land.
   (a) Which of these options would gather more rent in **one year**?
   (b) How much more?

Option One

6 blocks of 6 flats
24 terraced houses
32 semi-detached houses
18 small detached houses

Option Two

4 blocks of 8 flats
19 semi-detached houses
27 small detached houses
26 large detached houses

1 Spare parts for cars are shared equally among *Roadmaster* garages. How many of these parts are sent to each garage?

(a) 4545 tyres — 45 garages

(b) 2860 exhausts — 26 garages

(c) 4940 brake pads — 38 garages

(d) 5936 batteries — 56 garages

2 (a) 3496 ÷ 23   (b) 9982 ÷ 62   (c) 3618 ÷ 18

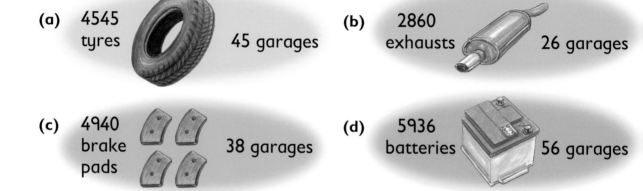

3 Some smaller parts are also shared equally among *Roadmaster* garages. How many of these parts are sent to each garage?

(a) 6820 bulbs — 31 garages

(b) 5535 spark plugs — 27 garages

(c) 4750 air filters — 19 garages

(d) 8990 fan belts — 29 garages

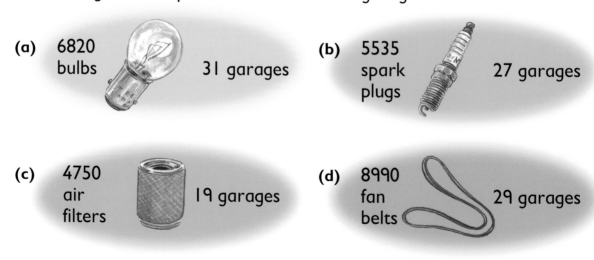

Seasalt Boating

Seasalt Boating		Boat Prices	
Mermaid	£3272	Seafoam	£33 836
Seagull	£6536	Neptune	£8352
Seaspray	£7650	Seashell	£5488
Shark	£20 160	Puffin	£41 792
Seacat	£9824	Seahorse	£4572
Gannet	£1908	Seashanty	£17 616

1 **(a)** Which of the boat prices are exactly divisible by 8?

(b) Copy and complete.

Prices (£s)exactly divisible by 8	3272						
Last 3 digits of the price	272						
Are the last 3 digits exactly divisible by 8?	Yes						

(c) Describe how you can check that a number is exactly divisible by 8.

2 **(a)** Which of these prices at *Seasalt Boating* are exactly divisible by 9?

£9855	£6804	£2080	£87 246	£47 849	£6531	£1422

£58 463	£2997	£14 170	£7362	£5179	£34 731	£969 318

(b) Copy and complete.

Prices (£s)exactly divisible by 9	9855						
Sum of the digits in the price	27						
Is the digit sum exactly divisible by 9?	Yes						

(c) Describe how you can check that a number is exactly divisible by 9.

3 Which of these numbers are
- exactly divisible by 8
- **not** exactly divisible by 9?

8856	24 632	3564	59 904	32 178	7424

1 Robert uses candles to make patterns of triangles.

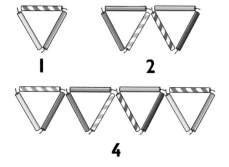

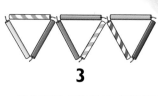

(a) Copy and complete this table:

Number of triangles	Number of candles
1 →	3
2 →	
3 →	
4 →	
5 →	

(b) How many candles are needed for
- 10 triangles
- 100 triangles?

(c) Copy and complete this rule:

The number of candles is ____ times the number of triangles.

2 Robert also makes patterns of rhombuses.

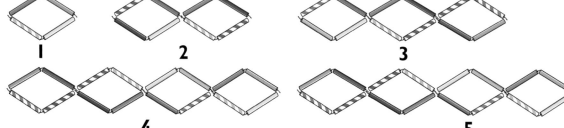

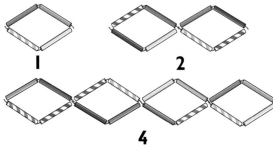

(a) Copy and complete this table:

Number of rhombuses	Number of candles
1 →	4
2 →	
3 →	
4 →	
5 →	

(b) How many candles are needed for
- 10 rhombuses
- 50 rhombuses?

(c) Copy and complete this rule:

The number of candles is ____ times the number of rhombuses.

(d) How many **rhombuses** can be made using
- 32 candles
- 80 candles?

1 Robert makes these patterns of squares.

(a) Copy and complete this table:

(b) Write a rule for finding
- the number of candles when you know the number of squares
- the number of squares when you know the number of candles.

Number of squares	Number of candles
1 →	4
2 →	
3 →	
4 →	
5 →	
8 →	
11 →	

2 In these patterns Robert also uses chocolate drops.

  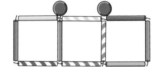 

(a) Draw a table to show the **Number of squares** and the **Number of drops** when there are 1, 2, 3, 4, 6, 9 and 15 squares.

(b) Write a rule for finding
- the number of drops when you know the number of squares
- the number of squares when you know the number of drops.

(c) How many squares are there when there are ● 19 drops ● 99 drops?

3

(a) Draw a table to show the **Number of triangles** and the **Number of drops** when there are 1, 2, 3, 4, 7, 10 and 21 triangles.

(b) Write a rule for finding
- the number of drops when you know the number of triangles
- the number of triangles when you know the number of drops.

(c) How many triangles are there when there are ● 52 drops ● 101 drops?

1 At the Children's Farm there is 1 goose for every 3 hens.
There are 5 geese. How many hens are there?

2 The farm has 1 horse for every 4 dogs.
There are 12 dogs. How many horses are there?

3 There are 3 cats for every 2 goats.
There are 6 cats. How many goats are there?

4 Rachael feeds some animals turnips and carrots.
Find the missing numbers in the table.

Animal	Ratio of turnips to carrots	Number of turnips	carrots
Horse	1 turnip to 3 carrots	6	**(a)**
Goat	3 turnips to 1 carrot	**(b)**	5
Donkey	2 turnips to 3 carrots	6	**(c)**
Sheep	3 turnips to 5 carrots	**(d)**	10

5 Three in every five eggs laid by the hens are brown. The rest are white.
Find the number of eggs of each colour when the number laid is

    (a) 15   **(b)** 25   **(c)** 50   **(d)** 30.

1 At the farm, 2 rabbits in every 3 are long-haired.
There are 12 rabbits altogether.
How many are   **(a)** long haired   **(b)** not long-haired?

2 4 in every 7 goats are male. There are 14 goats altogether.
How many are   **(a)** male   **(b)** female?

3 Rachael gives a total of 24 kilograms of feed to the goats
and sheep. She gives the sheep 1 kg in every 4 kg of feed.
What weight of feed is given to   **(a)** the goats   **(b)** the sheep?

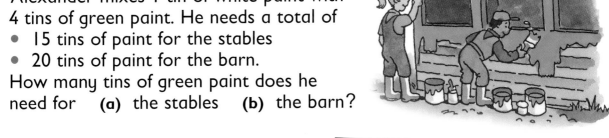

4 Alexander mixes 1 tin of white paint with
4 tins of green paint. He needs a total of
  • 15 tins of paint for the stables
  • 20 tins of paint for the barn.
How many tins of green paint does he
need for   **(a)** the stables   **(b)** the barn?

5 The table shows the numbers of larger
animals at the farm last year.
In simplest form, what was the ratio of

(a) horses to pigs
(b) sheep to cows
(c) horses to goats
(d) cows to pigs
(e) horses to **animals**
(f) pigs to animals?

Hillburn Children's Farm Numbers of larger animals	
Horses	6
Sheep	16
Goats	18
Pigs	12
Cows	8
	60

1 **(a)** Find the cost of 8 single tins.
   (b) Does the multipack give better value for money? Explain.

£1·34   multipack £10·16

2 How much does **one** tin of beans cost in
   (a) the family pack
   (b) the economy pack?
   Which pack gives better value?

family pack
£2·58

economy pack
£4·14

3 Which pack gives better value? Explain each time.

(a)

economy pack
£8·56

triple pack
£6·15

(b)

£6·75

£9·10

4 Dave makes up multipacks for *Price Co*. He decides their prices by taking one sixth off each **total** cost of buying several single items. What price would Dave make each of these multipacks?

(a)

(b)

(c)

single box costs £1·53   single packet costs £1·08   single bottle costs £3·16

5 What is the cost of
   (a) 5 cans   **(b)** 1 can
   (c) 4 boxes **(d)** 1 box?

50 cans
£38·50

40 boxes
£15·20

1 **(a)** Find the total time taken by each player to complete the *Reaction Time* event.

(b) What was the total time taken by each team to complete
  - Round 1
  - Round 2?

Reaction Time	Round 1 seconds	Round 2 seconds
Jack	0·426	0·513
Zoë	0·532	0·645
Gemma	0·704	0·861
Pete	0·650	0·928

2

Ring the Bell	Round 1 seconds	Round 2 seconds
Jack	3·434	3·052
Zoë	4·561	4·725
Gemma	2·342	3·647
Pete	3·136	4·213

For the *Ring the Bell* game,
(a) how long did each team take to complete
  - Round 1
  - Round 2?

(b) what was the total time taken by each player to complete both rounds?

3 The player in each team with the **lower** total time for **both** events takes part in the challenge final.

Which two players reached the final?

0·669	4·768	8·463	0·987	2·232	4·836
5·617	0·425	7·579	8·283	0·786	4·143
1·525	2·959	0·342	5·857	6·362	0·413
0·251	3·351	4·525	0·578	6·695	7·471
9·555	0·897	3·434	3·737	0·234	9·688
8·976	7·194	0·303	2·412	1·648	0·112

1 **Play this game with a partner.**

 • In turn, choose a red number and a purple number, then find the difference between them.

 • If correct, score 1 point and cover the two numbers with counters.

 • If wrong, leave the numbers uncovered. You score no points.

 • Continue until all the red and purple numbers are covered.

2 Play the game again using

 (a) blue and orange numbers   (b) green and brown numbers.

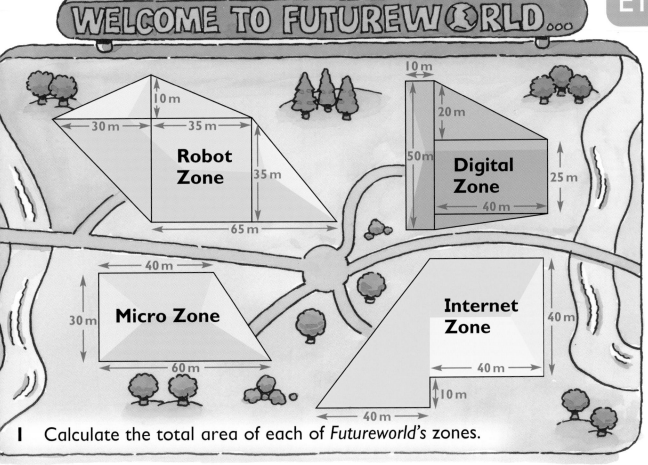

WELCOME TO FUTUREWORLD...

Robot Zone

10 m
30 m
35 m
35 m
65 m

Digital Zone

10 m
20 m
50 m
40 m
25 m

Micro Zone

40 m
30 m
60 m

Internet Zone

40 m
40 m
10 m
40 m

1 Calculate the total area of each of *Futureworld's* zones.

2 For each shape, **measure** side or other lengths then **calculate** the area.

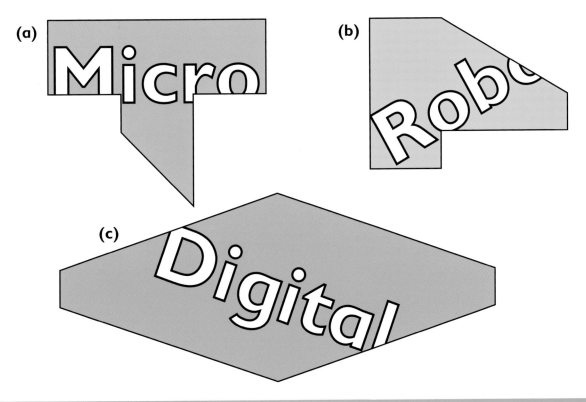

(a) Micro

(b) Robo

(c) Digital

1 At what time does each programme finish?

Programme	Starts	Lasts for
Daylight	07.21	46 min
Walkabout	10.43	51 min
House Call	13.16	63 min
Music Chart	19.14	1h 17 min
Nighthawk	21.38	1h 26 min
Motor Sport	22.56	1h 49 min

2 When does each programme start?

Programme	Fan Club	Seascape	Amazon Trek	Gardening life	Sportsweek
Lasts for	27 min	43 min	1h 34 min	1h 41 min	1h 56 min
Finishes	07.01	09.18	14.07	19.22	01.49

3 How many minutes does each programme last?

(a) *Wild World* starts at 08.58 and finishes at 10.06.

(b) *Quickquiz* starts at 11.49 and finishes at 13.01.

(c) *Spacewatch* starts at 14.16 and finishes at 15.43.

(d) *Comedy Capers* starts at 19.22 and finishes at 21.06.

(e) *Evening Drama* starts at 21.39 and finishes at 23.28.

(f) *Trading Post* starts at 23.41 and finishes at 01.39.

1   The Roving Reporter's name is Shareen.
    Her helicopter took off from its base at 06.19 on a 37 minute flight
    to Abercrombie Hall. When did it arrive?

2   Shareen's interview with Lady Abercrombie lasted for 1 hour and
    23 minutes. It finished at 08.41. When did the interview begin?

3   (a)   Shareen left Abercrombie Hall at 08.44 and arrived at the
          Botanic Gardens at 09.38.
          How long did the flight take?

    (b)   The film crew spent 116 minutes
          with the gardeners filming them
          building a new rock garden.
          At what time did they finish
          filming?

4   (a)   A picnic lunch for the gardeners
          and film crew started at 11.53.
          How long did the crew wait for lunch?

    (b)   Immediately after lunch Shareen flew to Morston to
          interview the mother of newly born quintuplets.
          The interview started at 14.28, 109 minutes after
          finishing lunch. How long did lunch last?

5   The interview at Morston took 34 minutes.
    The flight back to the helicopter base
    took 1 hour 14 minutes.

    (a)   When did the helicopter land?
    (b)   How long had Shareen been away from
          the helicopter base that day?

Each cuboid is built using centimetre cubes.

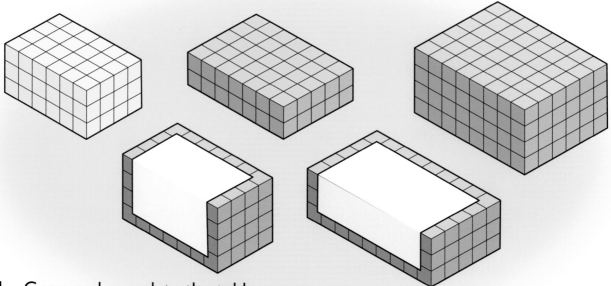

1 Copy and complete the table.

Cuboid	Number of cubes in one row (length)	Number of rows (breadth)	Numbers of layers (height)	Volume in centimetre cubes
Yellow	6	4	3	cm³

2 Write a rule to find the volume of a cuboid when you know its length, breadth and height.

3 Find the volume, in cm³, of each of these cuboids.

12 cm 4 cm 5 cm

7 cm 6 cm 5 cm

20 cm 4 c 12 cm

7 cm 8 cm 8 cm

10 cm 10 cm 10 cm

15 cm 6 cm 5 cm

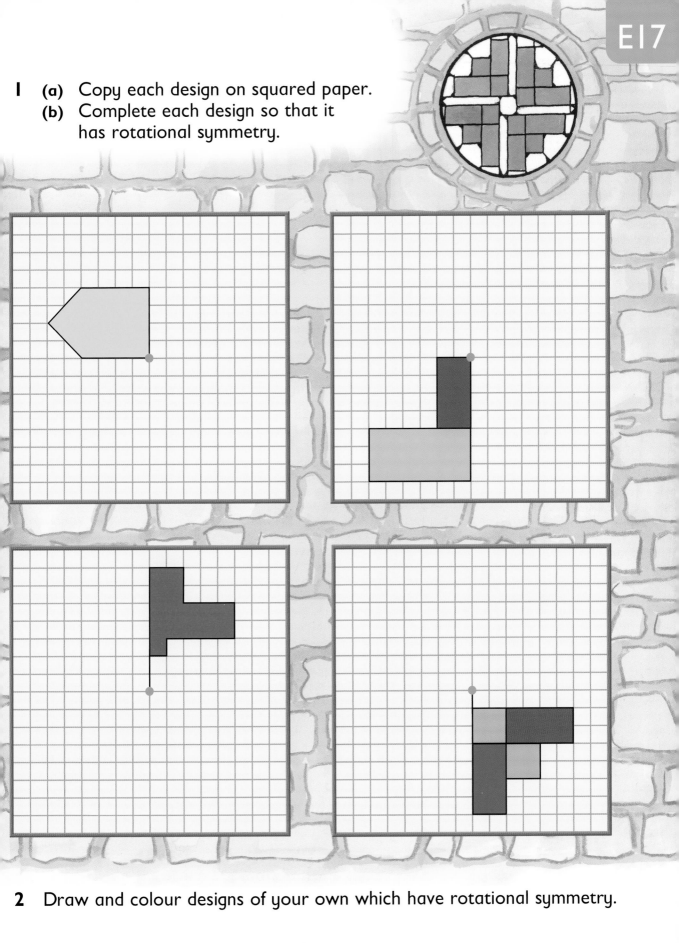

1 **(a)** Copy each design on squared paper.
(b) Complete each design so that it has rotational symmetry.

2 Draw and colour designs of your own which have rotational symmetry.

1 Draw a square with sides 10 cm long and vertices labelled A, B, C, D.

2 Mark a point
- 1 cm from A on side AB
- 1 cm from B on side BC
- 1 cm from C on side CD
- 1 cm from D on side DA.

3 Join up the points with straight lines to form a smaller square which is tilted.

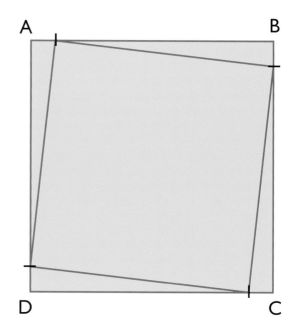

4 Repeat all of the above for the new, smaller square and then **repeat for each new square** formed to give:

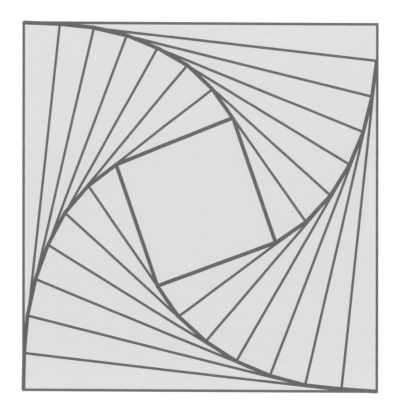

The curves which appear are called **pursuit curves**.

I Draw pursuit curves starting with a different shape each time.

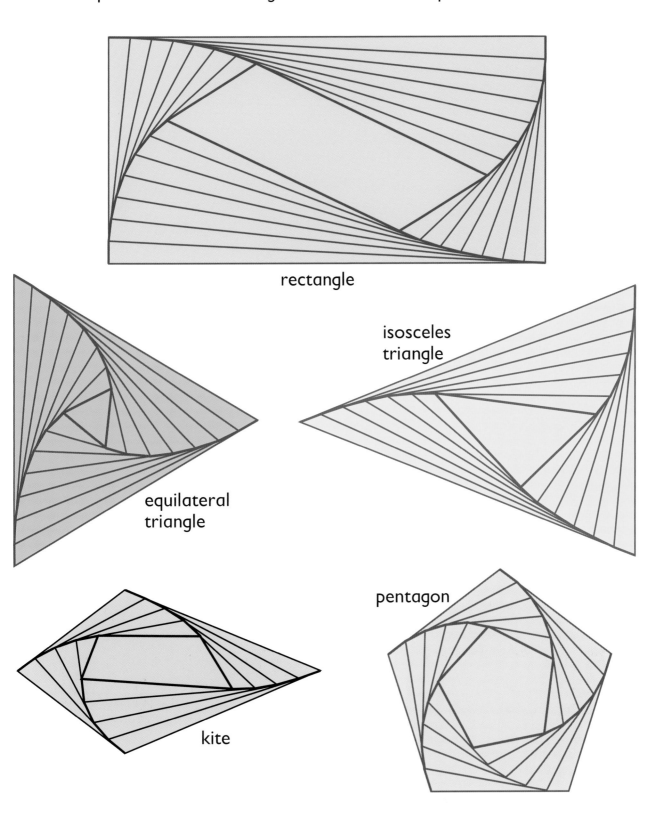

rectangle

equilateral triangle

isosceles triangle

kite

pentagon

2 Choose different starting shapes to draw other pursuit curves.

Use dotty paper.

1 Copy and continue each tiling.

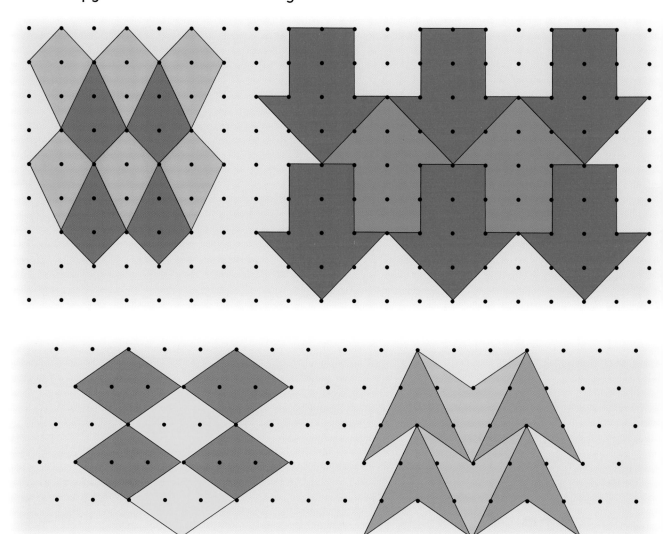

2 Make tilings using each of these shapes.

(a)   (b)

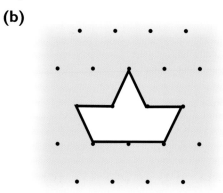

The point at which two lines cross each other is called an **intersection**.

When all the straight lines are drawn from 2 points to another 2 points there is only 1 intersection.

1 (a) How many intersections are there when the lines are drawn from 2 points to

- 3 points
- 4 points
- 5 points?

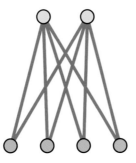
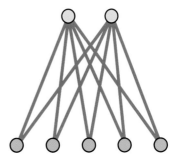

(b) Show your results in a table like this.

points lines drawn from	2	2	2	2
points lines drawn to	2	3	4	5
number of intersections	1			

2 Look for a pattern in the numbers in the table.
Use the pattern to **predict** how many intersections there are when the lines are drawn from 2 points to

(a) 6 points **(b)** 7 points **(c)** 8 points **(d)** 9 points **(e)** 10 points.

Use tracing paper if you need to.

1 List the co-ordinates of
- the vertices of each half shape
- the vertices needed to complete the shape so that the **red** line is an axis of symmetry.

(a)

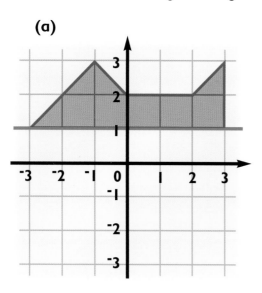

(b)

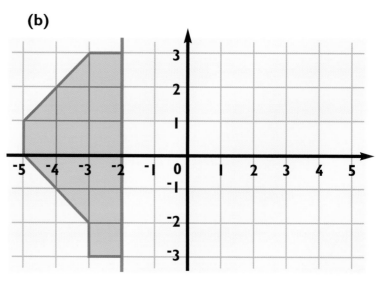

(c)

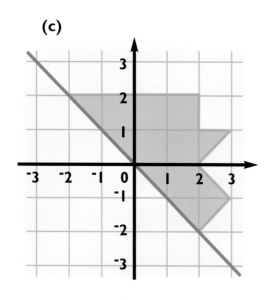

2 List the co-ordinates of
- the vertices of the shape
- the vertices of the shape's reflections when **both** red lines are axes of symmetry.

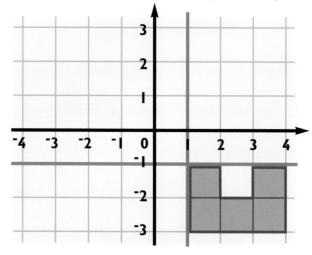

1 The pie chart shows the methods used by Class 6 to do a division calculation.

   (a) Which method was used by
- the greatest number of children
- the smallest number of children?

   (b) What **fraction** of the children used
- a written method
- a mental method
- a calculator method?

Method used

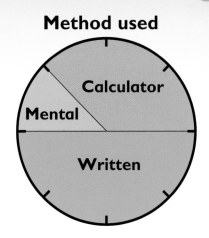

2 **Preferred subject**

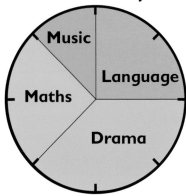

The pie chart shows which four subjects the children in Class 6 preferred.

Write True or False for each statement.

   (a) Music was preferred by the smallest number of children.

   (b) More than half the children preferred Drama.

   (c) Fewer children preferred Maths than Language.

   (d) Music and Drama **together** were preferred by exactly half the children.

3 The pie chart shows the favourite Maths topics of **ten** children in Class 6.

   (a) How many equal parts are there in the circle?

   (b) How many children chose
- Number
- Shape
- Measure
- Data handling?

   (c) What **percentage** of the children chose
- Number
- Measure?

   (d) In simplest form, what **fraction** of the children chose
- Shape
- Data handling?

   (e) Which two topics **together** were chosen by exactly half the children?

Favourite Maths topics

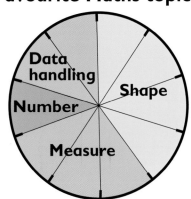

Bar line chart

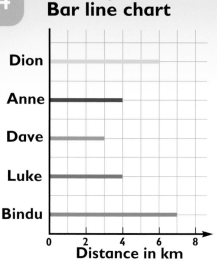

Dion
Anne
Dave
Luke
Bindu

0   2   4   6   8
Distance in km

Pie chart

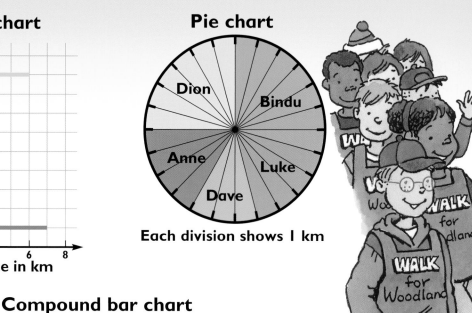

Each division shows 1 km

Compound bar chart

Bindu   Luke   Dave   Anne   Dion

6 km   12 km   18 km   24 km

1 Each of the three graphs shows the same information about the distances covered in a sponsored walk by children in the Red group.

Use any of the graphs.

(a) Which two children walked the same distance?
(b) What was the total distance walked by the group?
(c) Who walked one quarter of the total distance?
(d) What distance did each child walk?
(e) Which two children **together** walked more than half of the total distance?

2 For each part of question 1, which graph shows the answer most clearly?

3 Show the information in this pie chart in the form of
(a) a compound bar chart
(b) a **vertical** bar line chart.

4 Sponsors paid £1·50 for each kilometre walked.
How much money altogether was collected by the Blue group?

Sponsored walk - Blue group

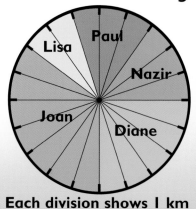

Lisa   Paul

Nazir

Joan

Diane

Each division shows 1 km

This straight-line graph shows the relationship between Pounds (£) and Euros (€) in 2002.

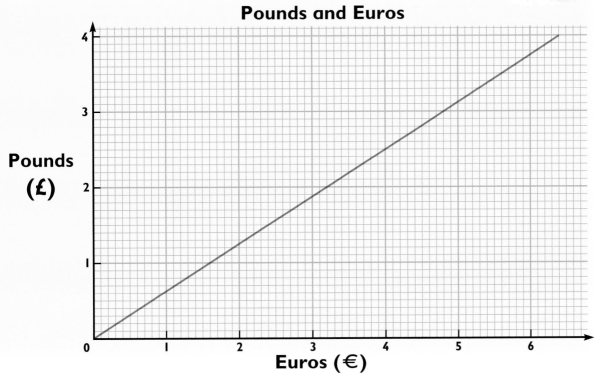

Pounds and Euros

Pounds (£)

Euros (€)

1 There are 100 cents in 1 Euro. What does each small interval represent
   (a) on the Euros axis   **(b)** on the Pounds axis?

2 Use the graph.
   ● Change to Euros.   **(a)** £1·00   **(b)** £3·50   **(c)** £2·25
   ● Change to Pounds.   **(d)** €4·00   **(e)** €2·40   **(f)** €6·00

3 In most European countries distances between towns are given in kilometres.
   ● Copy this graph on 2 mm squared paper.
   ● Extend one axis to 55 miles, the other to 90 km.
   ● Plot the points (32 km, 20 miles) and (80 km, 50 miles).
   ● Draw a line through these points to the origin to complete a straight-line graph.

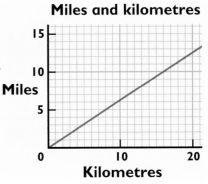

Miles and kilometres

Miles

Kilometres

4 Use your graph.
   ● Change to miles.   **(a)** 40 km   **(b)** 24 km   **(c)** 60 km
   ● Change to kilometres.   **(d)** 5 miles   **(e)** 30 miles   **(f)** 47·5 miles

1 **(a)** When a coin is tossed 50 times, how many times do you **think** it will show
- heads   • tails?

(b) Toss a coin 50 times. Record your results in a table like this:

Result	Tally marks	Frequency
Heads		
Tails		

2 **(a)** When a die is rolled 60 times, which number do you think will show
- most often   • least often?

(b) Roll a die 60 times. Record your results in a table like this:

Result	Tally marks	Frequency
1		
2		
3		
4		
5		
6		

(c) Are the results as you predicted? Explain.

3 **(a)**
- Place 1 red counter, 1 green counter and 1 blue counter in a bag.
- Without looking remove one of the counters.
- Record the colour of the counter in a frequency table then replace it.
- Repeat until you have 60 results.

(b) Are the results as you predicted? Explain.

1 **(a)** Make a 1–6 die using **Net A** from Pupil Sheet 60.

(b) Insert a drawing pin and cover it with sticky tape as shown.

(c) Roll the die 60 times. Record your results in a frequency table like this:

Result	Tally marks	Frequency
1		
2		
3		
4		

(d) Is the die fair? Explain.

2 **(a)** Make a 1–4 die using **Net B** from Pupil Sheet 60.

(b) Roll the die 40 times and each time record the hidden number in a frequency table.

(c) Is this die fair? Explain.

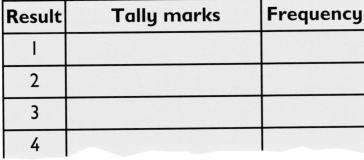

3 **(a)** Cut out the numbered hexagon from Pupil Sheet 60.

(b) Make a spinner by placing a pencil at the centre of the hexagon through a paper clip.

(c) Spin the paper clip 60 times. Record your results in a frquency table.

(d) Is the spinner fair? Explain.

1   Marston Bank first opened in the year 1750, when the town's population was 1000.
The population of Marston **doubled** every 25 years.

What was the population of Marston in the year 2000?

2   The total value of the tokens in the two bags is £2500.

How many tokens are   **(a)** red   **(b)** blue?

3

The secret number which opens the safe door is
- greater than 675
- less than 725
- a multiple of 5
- divisible by 3 **and** by 9.

What is the secret number?

4   Ten local bankers attend a meeting at Marston Bank.

Each banker shakes hands with **all** of the others.
How many handshakes are there altogether?

5
- A security van visits Marston Bank every 6 days.
- A fax from Head Office arrives every 15 days.
- The secret number which opens the safe is changed every 10 days.

One week, **all three** of these things happen on the **same** day.
After how many more days will all three things happen on the same day again?

  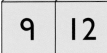

15 24	3 27	9 12	20 15

1 For which tile are **all** of these statements true?

- The product of the tile numbers is a three-digit number.
- The difference between the numbers is equal to one quarter of the larger number.
- Each number is a multiple of 3.

2 **(a)** Write a rule, involving multiplication and then subtraction, for using the numbers in the circles to make each number in the centre.

(b) Write a **different** rule for using the numbers in these circles to make each number in the centre.
Find the missing numbers.

3

A magician has a box of tricks.
There are fewer than 100 tricks in his box.

When I count in fives there are no tricks left over.
When I count in sixes there is one trick left over.
When I count in sevens there is still one left over.

How many tricks are in the magician's box?

4 START → square → double → ÷10 → FINISH

Which number from 1 to 10 can go through these three machines and be
(a) **the same** at the FINISH as it was at the START
(b) **twice as large** at the FINISH as it was at the START?

1   These are the values, **in U.S. dollars per ounce**, of three precious metals.

Gold	Silver	Platinum
$ 293·90	$ 4·40	$ 453

When one U.S. dollar is worth about seventy pence, what, **in U.K. pounds,** is

(a)   the approximate value of one ounce of
 • gold   • silver   • platinum

(b)   the approximate **total** value of ten ounces of gold, nine ounces of silver and twelve ounces of platinum

(c)   the difference between the approximate values of five ounces of platinum and eleven ounces of gold?

2   The value of **one kilogram**
 • of gold is £6570   • of platinum is £10 611.

What is the value of

(a) $\frac{1}{4}$ kg of gold   (b) $\frac{3}{5}$ kg of platinum

(d) $\frac{3}{4}$ kg of platinum **and** $1\frac{1}{10}$ kg of gold?

3   The values of gold and platinum fell by 10%. What is the new value of each of these precious metals?

4

Diamonds are weighed in **carats**.
1 carat = 0·2 grams

The Cullinan Diamond is the largest diamond ever found. It weighs 3015 carats.
(a)   What is the weight, in grams, of the Cullinan Diamond?
(b)   The value of a one-carat diamond is 10173 U.S. dollars.
 What is the approximate value of the Cullinan Diamond **in pounds**?